My Confirmation Journal

Love
Joy
Peace
Self-control
Patience
Kindness
Generosity
Faithfulness
Gentleness

AUTHORS

SISTERS OF NOTRE DAME

CHARDON, OHIO

LOYOLA PRESS.
A JESUIT MINISTRY

Contributing writers: Paul Campbell, S.J.; Jennon Bell Hoffmann

Cover design: Loyola Press

Cover illustration:
© iStockphoto.com/Tolga_TEZCAN (ribbon),
Mackey Creations/Shutterstock.com (dove),
iStockphoto/Thinkstock (background)

Interior design: Kathryn Seckman Kirsch

ISBN-13: 978-0-8294-3685-3
ISBN-10: 0-8294-3685-5

LOYOLA PRESS.
A JESUIT MINISTRY

3441 N. Ashland Avenue
Chicago, Illinois 60657
(800) 621-1008
www.loyolapress.com

12 13 14 15 16 17 18 19 RRD 10 9 8 7 6 5 4 3 2 1

This Journal belongs to

.......................Jody   Connors......................

who is preparing to be confirmed in the Spirit.

Name of parish

....

Name of pastor

....

contents

prayer

Prayer to the Holy Spirit

Come, Holy Spirit, fill the hearts of your faithful.

And kindle in them the fire of your love.

Send forth your Spirit and they shall be created.

And you shall renew the face of the earth.

Let us pray:

O God, by the light of the Holy Spirit you have taught the hearts of your faithful. In the same Spirit, help us to know what is truly right and always to rejoice in your consolation. We ask this through Christ, Our Lord.

Amen.

My Journey Begins

My name is Jody Genevieve Francis Connors.

I like my name because . . .

Genevieve was my Grammy's name.

Some interesting facts about me are . . .

I love dance, art, and music. I go to De La Salle. I was born on January 28th, 2004. I am 12. I love school!

This is my self-portrait.

Important people in my life are . . .

my mom, my dad, Barbie, my friends,

My best friend is .... **because . . .**

When people think of me, I hope the following things come to mind:

kind, smart, creative, loving, helpful, faithful

My favorite book is .... **because . . .**

....

....

....

....

My favorite movie is .... **because . . .**

....

....

....

....

My favorite song or musician is .... **because . . .**

....

....

....

....

Some activities I like to do for fun are . . .

Dance

When I am alone, I like to . . .

Dance

When I need to let off steam, I . . .

Dance

This is a drawing of how I feel right now.

My favorite activity to do with friends is . . .

bowl, do art, shop, dance, anything.

Some of my interests include . . .

Dance, art, writing, design,

because . . .

They allow me to express myself.

Some things I dislike are . . .

Sports, fruit,

When I become an adult, I want to . . .

Fashion Design.

Use this time line to set goals for your future.

Everyone can help make the world a better place by . . .

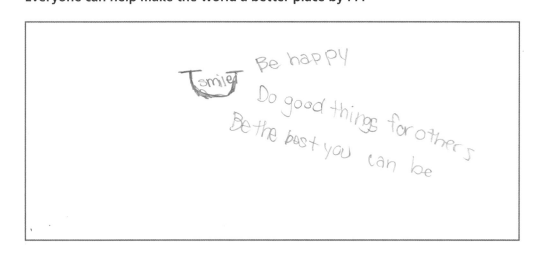

Be happy
Do good things for others
Be the best you can be

Some dreams or goals for myself are . . .

....

....

....

Some dreams or goals for my family are . . .

....

....

....

Some dreams or goals for the world and society are . . .

....

....

....

As I begin my preparation for Confirmation, my expectations are . . .

....

....

....

....

....

strength

strength

A promise means . . .

....

....

....

A promise I am willing to make and keep is . . .

....

....

....

2

Once when I was lost . . .

....

....

....

When the experience was over, I . . .

....

....

....

Annunciation, He Qi, 2001.

How is God inviting me to say yes to the Lord, as Mary did?

....

....

....

....

....

....

....

....

....

My family works as a team by . . .

4

I can show kindness to others by . . .

When I'm having a rough day, I find comfort and strength in . . .

....

....

....

....

....

....

....

My friends are important because . . .

....

....

....

....

....

....

....

Some words I can say to comfort and support others are . . .

Prayer

I'm thankful to God for . . .	I ask God to fill my heart with . . .

I can show my love for God and others by . . .

My reflections

My reflections

belonging

belonging

The five things I can't live without are . . .

They are important because . . .

....

....

....

....

....

....

The last time I disobeyed my parents or teacher, I remedied the situation by . . .

....

....

....

....

How do my family and friends help me know God's love?

....

....

....

Where have I discovered the face of God during this time of preparation
for Confirmation?

....

....

....

....

....

....

....

....

....

Evensong, Margaret Baird, oil on board, 1972.

My personality traits and qualities that I think stand out the most are . . .

....

....

....

....

....

....

....

14

I would want to be friends with me because . . .

....

....

....

....

....

....

....

....

I belong to . . .

....

....

....

....

....

....

....

....

....

15

....

....

....

....

....

....

....

....

I am fulfilling my baptismal promises to God in the following ways . . .

....

....

....

....

....

....

....

16

As I prepare for Confirmation, I profess to God and others the following . . .

If I could invent something that would help solve a crisis or problem happening in the world today, I would invent . . .

....

....

....

....

....

my invention

Prayer

Imagine your favorite place. Then imagine you're there, and Jesus is with you. Jesus looks at you expectantly. What would you say to him? What do you think he'd say to you?

My reflections

My reflections

identity

identity

My favorite quote, saying, or music lyric is . . .

....

....

....

I find it significant because . . .

....

....

....

Five things I like about myself are . . .

1. ....

2. ....

3. ....

4. ....

5. ....

When I need help and support, I . . .

....

....

....

Describe some simple ways you find God in your daily life.

....

....

....

....

....

....

....

....

Jesus our High Priest, through the Holy Spirit, draws us into the Father's love, Elizabeth Wang, 2010.

Values or beliefs I have learned from my family are . . .

....

....

....

....

....

....

....

What I admire most about my parents or guardians is . . .

....

....

....

....

....

....

....

....

My vision of a perfect world is . . .

A creed or motto is a guiding principle or statement of belief. My personal creed is . . .

We can find small acts in our everyday lives that we want to applaud. A recent event that made me want to stand up and cheer was when . . .

Think about your brother or sister, or if you do not have siblings, a relative with whom you share a close bond. What are some of his or her special qualities?

Prayer

Think about your core values, what matters most to you. Five statements that reflect what I believe at this moment in my life are . . .

My reflections

My reflections

action

action

Well-known sayings such as "An apple a day keeps the doctor away" or "Never go to bed angry" are guidelines for a happy and healthy life. What is your favorite saying? Why?

Think about the laws that govern our society. Why are they necessary? What laws would you like to change, institute, or eliminate for future generations?

How have I personally experienced the "tug" of making a good decision?

....

....

....

....

....

....

....

....

....

....

Denial, Stevie
Taylor, 1999.

Having free will means . . .

....

....

....

....

....

....

....

....

34

Free will affects my choices in the following ways . . .

....

....

....

....

....

....

....

....

....

Think about the concept of paying it forward, whereby one good deed leads to another. Draw a comic strip illustrating the idea of paying it forward.

> **Writer and humorist Sam Levenson has been quoted as saying, "As you grow older, you will discover that you have two hands: one for helping yourself, the other for helping others."**

Recently, I helped someone by . . .

....

....

....

....

....

....

The last time someone helped me was . . .

....

....

....

....

....

....

Blessed Teresa of Calcutta chose to live and work among the impoverished and those deprived of their rights in Calcutta, India.

A cause close to my heart is . . .

....

....

....

....

....

....

This cause is important because . . .

....

....

....

....

....

....

....

....

Prayer

Special intentions are people or issues that you keep in mind while praying.

Who or what are your special intentions lately?

Write a short prayer for your special intentions.

My reflections

My reflections

talents

talents

A talent or ability that I'm most proud of is . . .

....

....

....

A way I can use my talent to help others is . . .

....

....

....

The skill or personal aspect I would most like to improve or acquire is . . .

....

....

....

It's important to better myself this way because . . .

....

....

....

Describe a time when all the pieces fit together in your life, when you felt especially together or whole.

43

Lamentation pour Haiti, Tamara Natalie Madden, United States, 21st century.

Ten qualities a best friend should possess are . . .

1. ....

2. ....

3. ....

4. ....

5. ....

6. ....

7. ....

8. ....

9. ....

10. ....

These qualities are necessary because . . .

....

....

....

....

....

....

....

....

Who is someone you look up to and why?

....

....

....

....

....

....

....

....

How can you emulate this person in your own life?

....

....

....

....

....

....

....

....

Draw a few symbols that represent you and explain what they tell about you.

Saint Catherine of Siena described her experience of praying to God like swimming in the sea, deep and open.

What element of nature do you associate with God? Why?

Prayer

Think of the gifts in your life, the people who love you, and the life you lead.
Write a thanksgiving prayer to God.

My reflections

My reflections

healer

healer

Think about yourself as a child. Did you have a favorite toy, or a special article of clothing? An item that meant a lot to me as a child was . . .

....

....

Now that I'm older, that same item . . .

....

....

Think about a close friend. What traits do you have in common?

....

....

....

In what ways do you differ?

....

....

....

How do your similarities and differences bring you closer?

....

....

....

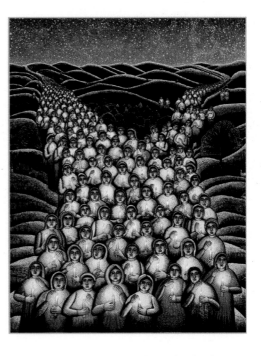

Festival of Lights, John August Swanson, 1991.

Write your name in the middle of the relationship web below. Then think about those connected to you. Around your name, write the names of people or things that matter most to you.

The people and things in my relationship web have shaped my life by . . .

....

....

....

....

Every person has his or her own way of coping with stress or difficult times.

Something that lifts my spirits is . . .

....

....

....

....

....

....

When I'm stressed, I can turn to . . .

....

....

....

....

....

....

A time that I had to forgive myself was when . . .

Think about the word *forgiveness* and what it means to you. How did it feel when you received forgiveness from someone you wronged? What was it like when someone asked you for forgiveness?

What are you passionate about? If you could do any one thing for the rest of your life, what would you do? How can you make this passion a reality?

Prayer

Admitting when I'm wrong is . . .

My reflections

My reflections

maturity

maturity

A person of importance in my life is . . .

....

This person is important because . . .

....

....

....

....

Every person has the ability to be an everyday superhero. What is your talent or power? How do you use it to help the community and those around you?

....

....

....

....

....

....

....

....

....

The Last Supper (detail), Gaston de La Touche, 1897.

How do I accept my responsibility to lead and serve others, as Jesus does for me?

Gifts from the heart can mean so much more than any material gift.

A gift I can give from my heart is . . .

Someone to whom I might give this gift is . . .

....

....

....

....

....

....

....

....

....

....

Jesus welcomes all of us into his Church. His only request is to live our lives as he did, loving the Father and caring for others.

I can live by Jesus' example in the following ways . . .

....

....

....

....

....

....

....

....

....

....

....

....

....

Imagine you are writing a letter that will be locked in a time capsule. What do you want future generations to know about you and your beliefs?

Think about the children of the world who are in need.

I can help children in need by . . .

....

....

....

....

....

....

....

....

....

....

....

....

....

....

....

....

67

Prayer

How will you live your life to your fullest potential?
What will help you be the best person you can be?

....

....

....

....

....

....

....

....

....

....

....

....

....

My reflections

My reflections

purpose

purpose

Many times we do something without focusing on the true purpose and meaning behind it. Think about a prayer that you pray often. What is this prayer really about?

....

....

....

....

What am I asking of God when I pray this prayer?

....

....

....

....

Reflecting honestly, whom or what in your life do you take for granted? What actions could you take to show your appreciation?

....

....

....

....

....

....

Saint Ignatius of Loyola teaches that love is shown more in deeds than in words. What particular deeds will you undertake after celebrating the Sacrament of Confirmation?

....

....

....

....

....

....

....

....

....

....

....

....

....

....

....

Mary of Pentecost, Cerezo Barredo, 1994.

A ritual in my life is . . .

....

....

....

....

....

....

....

....

This ritual is important because . . .

....

....

....

....

....

....

....

....

Imagine that people wore labels on their clothes that identified positive qualities about them. What would your labels say?

Who are some people you know (either famous or personally) who share these qualities? How?

....

....

....

....

....

....

Think about a time you woke up energized and ready to start the day. That feeling of excitement and purpose can help us accomplish many things. As a follower of Jesus, what can you do to help spread the Good News?

Like Saint Ignatius of Loyola, I find God in all things because . . .

....

....

....

....

....

....

....

....

....

....

....

....

....

....

Prayer

Where do you see yourself in five years? In 10 years?
Where does God fit in your life plan?

....

....

....

....

....

....

....

....

....

....

....

....

....

....

....

....

....

....

My reflections

....

....

....

....

....

....

....

....

....

....

....

....

....

....

My reflections

My Confirmation Day

I received the Sacrament of Confirmation on .... of
(date)

.... by .... at ....
(year)   (name of bishop)   (name of parish)

I chose .... as my sponsor because . . .

....

Some ways my sponsor and I prepared for Confirmation are . . .

....

....

Here's a photo of my sponsor and me.

81

My Confirmation name is .... in honor of Saint

....

I chose this name because . . .

....

....

....

Some interesting facts about this saint are . . .

....

....

....

This is what my saint looks like:

Before I began to prepare for the Sacrament of Confirmation, I felt . . .

....

....

Now I feel . . .

....

....

The Gifts and Fruits of the Holy Spirit will help me . . .

....

....

....

Write a prayer to God below.

Acknowledgments

Photography credits: iv © iStockphoto.com/tuja66. **iv** © iStockphoto.com/tuja66. **v** Comstock/Thinkstock. **1** © iStockphoto.com/vesilvio. **3** He Qi, He Qi Arts, www.heqigallery.com. **5** iStockphoto/Thinkstock. **9** © iStockphoto/Tolga_TEZCAN. **11** © iStockphoto.com/epicurean. **13** Private Collection/The Bridgeman Art Library International. **15** © iStockphoto.com/Creative_Improv. **21** © William Voon/Veer. **23** Image by Elizabeth Wang, RL Code T-05121-CW-V3, © Radiant Light 2010, www.radiantlight.org.uk. **31** Jimmy Lopes/Hemera/Thinkstock. **33** Private Collection/The Bridgeman Art Library International. **34** © iStockphoto.com/petekarici. **41** © iStockphoto.com/mitza. **43** Private Collection/The Bridgeman Art Library International. **51** © iStockphoto.com/Jasmina007. **53** Festival of Lights, Copyright 2000 by John August Swanson, Serigraph 30 ¾" x 24", www.JohnAugustSwanson.com, Los Angeles artist John August Swanson is noted for his finely detailed, brilliantly colored paintings and original prints. His works are found in the Smithsonian Institution's National Museum of American History, London's Tate Gallery, the Vatican Museum's Collection of Modern Religious Art, and the Bibliothèque Nationale, Paris. **61** javarman/Shutterstock.com. **63** Hermitage, St. Petersburg, Russia/The Bridgeman Art Library International. **71** Kelly Nelson/Shutterstock.com. **73** M. Cerezo Barredo. Mary of Pentecost, mural in the curia of the Claretian Missionaries, Rome, 1994. **74** © iStockphoto.com/Creative_Improv.